D0900115

To the
Fischer family
Happy New Year
5728
Rabbi & Elaine Asa

A BOOK OF TORAH READINGS

A BOOK OF TORAH READINGS

by MORRIS EPSTEIN

paintings by
EZEKIEL SCHLOSS

KTAV PUBLISHING HOUSE, INC.

Designed by EZEKIEL SCHLOSS

Library of Congress Catalog Card Number 60 11069

KTAV PUBLISHING HOUSE, INC.

TABLE OF CONTENTS

To

the sacred memory

of my

revered parents

GITTEL

and

ISAAC

ת׳נ׳צ׳ב׳ה׳

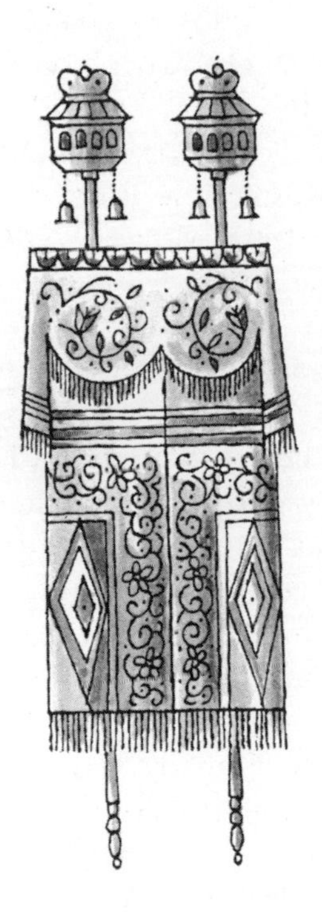

READING THE TORAH

We are commanded by the Torah itself to study its teachings. "You shall teach these words to thy children; you shall talk of them in your house, and when you walk by the way, when you lie down, and when you rise," we are told in *Deuteronomy* 6:6-7.

When Moses bade farewell to the Israelites before his death, he instructed them to read the Torah at the end of every seventh year, on the festival of Sukkot. It was not, however, until the time of Ezra (about 500 B.C.E.) that the regular reading of the Torah in the synagogue was begun. To remind his people of the great lessons in the Torah, Ezra assembled them and read the Scriptures to them.

Part of the Synagogue Service

Slowly, the reading of the Torah became a basic part of the synagogue service. Portions were read on festivals and Sabbaths, and on Mondays and Thursdays, the market-days when the rural population came to the cities. This was followed by the introduction of the Haftarah, the selection from the Prophets that is read at the conclusion of the weekly portion.

When the Temple was destroyed and sacrifices were replaced by prayers, many Bible passages were included in the service. The Offering of Isaac, the Song of Moses at the Red Sea, the chapters of the Shema, are a few examples.

The Cycles and the Sidrot

In the synagogue the reading of the Torah took on two forms. One was an annual cycle in which the Five Books of Moses were read every year. This system is the one in universal use today. Another custom was to read the Torah in a period of three years.

The first system divided the Torah into fifty-four *sidrot*. The term *sidra* at first meant "arrangement," but was later applied to the actual Sabbath or festival portion read in the synagogue.

The *sidrot* are not divided as such in the Torah Scroll, but are exactly defined in traditional sources. The names of the *sidrot* derive from their first word or two (Berayshis, Lekh Lekha) or from the first important word (Kedoshim). Sometimes, the significant word is the name of the principal character in the story (Pinhas, Noah, Balak).

Originally, everyone who was called to the Torah read his own part of the *sidra*, but it grew difficult to find laymen able to read from the Scroll, and it became customary to engage a professional reader (Baal Kore).

When the closing sentence of any of the Five Books of Moses is reached, the congregation rises; the reader ends with a flourish in a loud voice, and the congregation exclaims "*hazak, hazak, venithazek*" ("Be strong, be strong, let us be strong!"), which the reader repeats.

The Traditional Chant

From the beginning, the readings from the Bible were rendered as a chant. By constant repetition, the chant and its notes became fixed and traditional. Over the centuries, a system of signs called "accents" (Hebrew: *ta'ame neginah*) was established. This system was perfected by Aaron ben Asher of Tiberias in the ninth century and became the standard code.

The Names of the Five Books

The Five Books of Moses (in Hebrew *Humash*, from *hamesh*, meaning "five") are often referred to as the "Pentateuch," from two Greek words meaning "five" and "tool" or "book." The following are the names generally used for the Five Books of Moses:

1. *Genesis,* from the Greek translation (*geneseos*) of the Hebrew word *toledot,* "generations," in *Genesis* 2:4. "These are the generations of the heavens and of the earth." The Hebrew name, *Berayshis,* "in the beginning" is taken from the first word of the Hebrew text, "In the beginning God created . . ."

2. *Exodus,* from the Greek translation of the Hebrew *Yetziat Mitzraim,* "exodus from Egypt." The Hebrew name, *Shemot,* "names," is derived from the first words of the book, *Ve-eleh Shemot,* "these are the names."

3. *Leviticus.* The name suggests that the book deals with matters concerning the Levites (and the priests). The Hebrew title, *Vayikra* ("and He called"), is the first word in the book.

4. *Numbers,* from the Greek *arithmoi,* translated into Latin as *numeri,* and then into English as "numbers." *Bemidbar* ("in the desert"), the Hebrew name, is the fifth word in the book, and justly describes the contents.

5. *Deuteronomy,* from the Greek *deuteronomion,* a translation of the Hebrew *Mishneh Torah,* "repetition of the law." The Hebrew

name for this book is *Devarim,* "the words," from the opening verse: "These are the words."

* * *

As the cycle of Torah-reading is endless, so is the teaching of Bible without beginning or end. It is hoped that the brief content-descriptions of the fifty-four *sidrot* that follow will weave a strand of love born of knowledge between youngsters and the Bible; that Torah readings in the synagogue will become more meaningful to them; and that they will be drawn to study the Torah itself.

For thus are links forged in the chain of time-honored tradition, and thus, to paraphrase the precept, do we "teach these words to our children."

—MORRIS EPSTEIN

THE TORAH BLESSINGS

BLESSINGS BEFORE READING THE TORAH

בָּרְכוּ אֶת־יְיָ הַמְבֹרָךְ׃

BLESS YE THE LORD WHO IS TO BE BLESSED

בָּרוּךְ יְיָ הַמְבֹרָךְ לְעוֹלָם וָעֶד׃

CONG.—Blessed be the Lord Who is to be blessed, for ever and ever.

בָּרוּךְ אַתָּה יְיָ, אֱלֹהֵינוּ מֶלֶךְ הָעוֹלָם,
אֲשֶׁר בָּחַר בָּנוּ מִכָּל הָעַמִּים
וְנָתַן לָנוּ אֶת תּוֹרָתוֹ. בָּרוּךְ אַתָּה
יְיָ, נוֹתֵן הַתּוֹרָה.

The response is repeated and the blessings continued:—

Blessed art Thou, O Lord our God, King of the universe, Who hast chosen us from all peoples, and hast given us Thy Torah. Blessed art Thou, O Lord, giver of the Torah.

BLESSINGS AFTER READING THE TORAH

בָּרוּךְ אַתָּה יְיָ, אֱלֹהֵינוּ מֶלֶךְ הָעוֹלָם,
אֲשֶׁר נָתַן לָנוּ תּוֹרַת אֱמֶת
וְחַיֵּי עוֹלָם נָטַע בְּתוֹכֵנוּ. בָּרוּךְ אַתָּה
יְיָ, נוֹתֵן הַתּוֹרָה.

Blessed art Thou, O Lord our God, King of the universe, Who hast given us the law of truth, and hast planted everlasting life in our midst. Blessed art Thou, O Lord, giver of the Torah.

THE SIDROT

בראשית

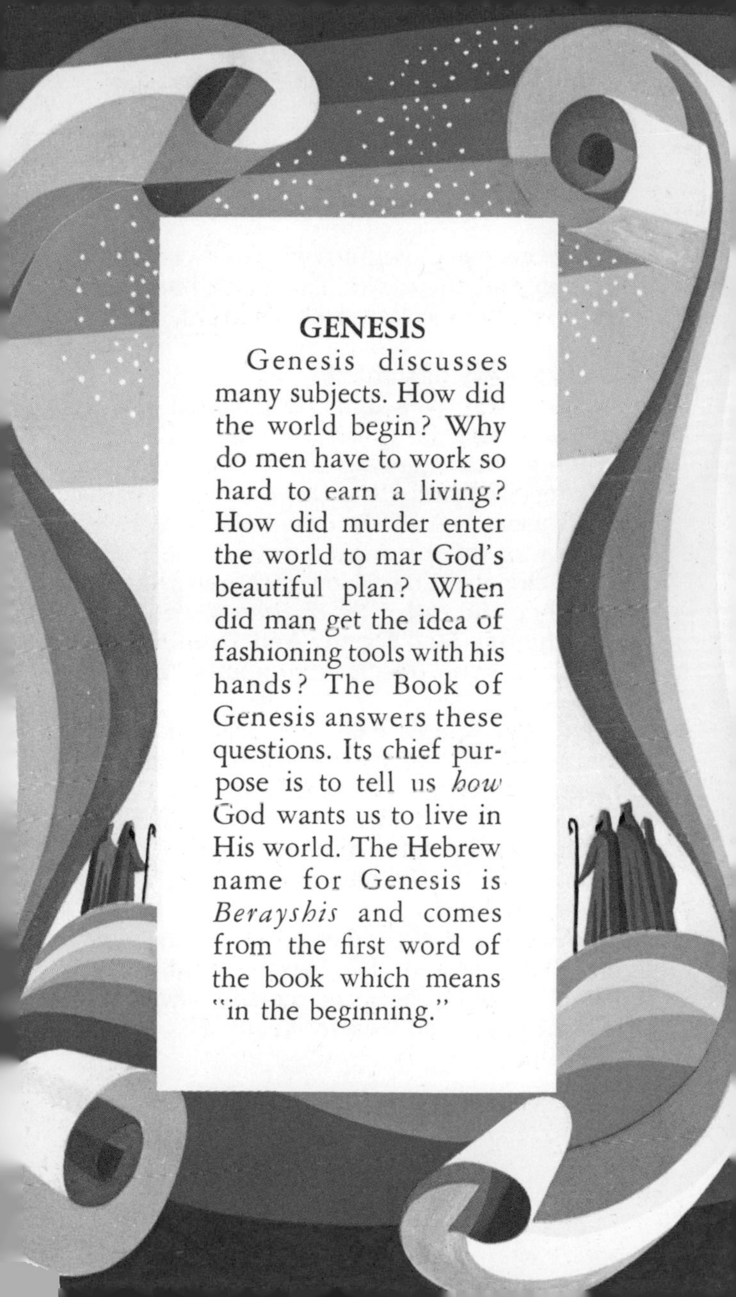

GENESIS

Genesis discusses many subjects. How did the world begin? Why do men have to work so hard to earn a living? How did murder enter the world to mar God's beautiful plan? When did man get the idea of fashioning tools with his hands? The Book of Genesis answers these questions. Its chief purpose is to tell us *how* God wants us to live in His world. The Hebrew name for Genesis is *Berayshis* and comes from the first word of the book which means "in the beginning."

B'RAYSHIS
בראשית

In the very beginning, God created the heaven and the earth. The earth had no form and darkness covered the waters. And God said:

"Let there be light!"

And there was light. God called the light Day and the darkness He called Night. And evening and morning made one day.

Then God said, "Let there be a sky between the waters." And He called the sky Heaven. That was on the second day.

On the third day, God gathered the waters together and called the gathered waters Seas, and the dry land Earth. And from the Earth sprouted fruit trees, and plants, and vegetables.

On the fourth day God created the Sun, and the Moon, and the stars, to give light upon the Earth. The fifth day saw the creation of fish that swim and birds that fly.

Then God created animals, reptiles and wild beasts and, finally, man and woman. That was the sixth day.

Thus was the world created. On the seventh day, God rested. He blessed that day and called it holy, because on the seventh day —Shabbat—God rested from His work of creation.

Genesis 1:1—6:8

NOAH
נֹחַ

Adam and Eve had children and grandchildren, and people multiplied upon the face of the earth. But they became wicked, until God was sorry that He had created man.

Only one man was worthy in the eyes of God, and that was Noah. So God said to Noah:

"I have decided to send a flood of water upon the earth to destroy every living thing. But I will save you and your family."

God instructed Noah in the making of an Ark, to be 450 feet long, 75 feet wide, and 45 feet high. Noah boarded the Ark with his wife and children and took along pairs of every sort of living thing with him, male and female of each kind, and food to keep them alive.

Then it rained for forty days and nights. Every living creature was drowned in the flood. And God remembered Noah. The waters went down and Noah stepped out on dry land.

God said in His heart: "I will never again destroy living things as I have done." God then spoke to Noah: "I set My rainbow in the clouds to be a symbol of My promise to you. Whenever I will look upon it, I will remember the everlasting agreement between Me and every living creature."

Genesis 6:9—11:32

LEKH LEKHA

לך לך

From Shem, Noah's eldest son, descended Terah, who was the father of Abram. Terah dwelt in the city of Haran.

After Abram's father Terah died, the Lord said to Abram: "Leave your father's house and go into a new land which I will show you. For I shall start a new nation with you."

So Abram and his wife Sarai left for Canaan. He took his nephew Lot, too.

At Shechem the Lord appeared to Abram again. He told Abram: "Unto your children will I give this land!" And Abram said: "I have no children!" Whereupon God replied: "Look up to the sky and count the stars if you can. So many shall be the number of your children and children's children. To them I shall give this land!"

When Abram was ninety-nine, God appeared once more to him and said: "Henceforth let your wife Sarai be called Sarah, for she shall be a princess by your side. And your name will be Abraham [father of many]. I will bless you both and give you a son, whose name will be Isaac. I will establish My covenant with Isaac and I will make you the father of a great people."

Genesis 12:1—17:27

VAYERA
וירא

One day, as Abraham sat in the door of his tent, he saw three strangers standing nearby. He ran to welcome them and said: "Please stay a while." He fetched water to wash their feet, and food for refreshment.

The three strangers were really angels, and one of them said: "Tell your wife Sarah that God will bless you both with a son."

God kept His promise. They had a son and named him Isaac. Later, to test Abraham's faith, the Lord said: "Abraham, take your dear son Isaac and offer him as a sacrifice to Me."

Sadly, Abraham obeyed. He brought Isaac to Mount Moriah, and prepared to do God's bidding. When the Lord saw that Abraham was true to Him, He caused a ram to appear, and ordered Abraham to substitute the ram for Isaac on the altar.

And God said: "Because you have obeyed without questioning, I will bless your children forever. Your descendants will be as numerous as the stars of the sky, and as the sands of the seashore."

From this experience of Abraham we learn that God forbade child-sacrifice. We also learn about the obedience and faith of Isaac, who proved himself worthy of carrying on the great mission of Abraham.

Genesis 18:1—22:24

HAYYE SARAH
חיי שרה

Sarah, Abraham's beloved wife, died. Abraham buried her in the cave of Machpelah in the land of Canaan.

Then Abraham told his servant Eliezer to go back to his native country and take a wife for his son Isaac from among his own relations.

With a caravan of ten camels, Eliezer came to the town of Nahor. He and his camels rested near the well. As the town maidens came to the well, Eliezer asked of them: "May I drink of the water in your pitcher?"

The first to reply was Rebekah, daughter of Bethuel, nephew of Abraham. She said: "Drink, sir, and I will draw water for your camels also."

When Eliezer learned who she was, he thanked God for His help. And Rebekah invited Eliezer to her home, where he met her father and her brother Laban.

They heard all that had happened and said: "This has been destined by the Lord. If Rebekah is willing, take her and let her be the wife of Isaac."

Rebekah gladly consented, and Eliezer returned with her. Isaac loved Rebekah and married her. And Abraham lived one hundred and seventy-five years. When he died he was buried in the cave of Machpelah, near Sarah his wife.

Genesis 23:1—25:18

TOLEDOT
תולדת

When Isaac was sixty years old, Rebekah bore him twin sons. The eldest was born ruddy and hairy, and was named Esau. The younger one held on to his brother's heel as he was born, and they called him Jacob.

The boys grew up and Esau was a cunning hunter who loved outdoor life. Jacob was a quiet person, serious and studious. Esau was Isaac's favorite, but Rebekah loved Jacob dearly.

One day Jacob cooked a thick soup. Esau, who had just returned from hunting, said: "I am starved. Feed me, my brother."

Jacob had thought about Esau's carefree attitude, and how Esau had neglected all his responsibilities. So he said: "Sell me your birthright first, and then I will feed you." (With Esau's birthright, Jacob would be the spiritual leader of his people.)

Esau agreed and swore to exchange his birthright for a bowl of soup.

When Isaac was old and almost blind, he called Esau to give him a father's blessing. But Rebekah disguised Jacob as Esau and Isaac blessed Jacob instead.

When Esau found out what had happened, he hated Jacob and plotted to kill him. So Rebekah ordered Jacob to flee to Laban, his uncle.

Genesis 25:19—28:9

VAYETZE
ויצא

Jacob left Beer-sheba. On the way to Haran, at sundown, Jacob lay down to sleep. He dreamed of a ladder reaching from earth to heaven, and God's angels went up and down the ladder.

Then God spoke to Jacob, saying: "This land will I give to your descendants. I will be with you and protect you wherever you go."

When Jacob arose in the morning, he said: "This must be God's House." And he called the place Beth-El—the House of God.

When Jacob came to Haran, he spent twenty years at the home of his uncle Laban. He married Laban's daughters, Leah and Rachel. Jacob's family increased; he became very rich and had large flocks. But he heard Laban's sons saying: "Jacob has gotten all his wealth from what our father had." So, after the birth of his son Joseph, Jacob left Haran, taking with him his family and his possessions.

Laban pursued Jacob, but the Lord appeared in a dream to Laban, cautioning him not to harm Jacob. Laban listened to the Lord and returned to Haran. Meanwhile Jacob continued on his journey back to Canaan.

Genesis 28:10—32:3

VAYISHLAH
וישלח

Jacob and his family journeyed on toward Canaan. One night a stranger came upon Jacob and began to wrestle with him. All night long they wrestled but the man could not defeat Jacob.

When day broke, Jacob knew that it was an angel of the Lord who had wrestled with him. The angel declared: "Jacob, you shall be called Israel from this day forth. 'Israel' means you have wrestled with God and have survived!"

Now Jacob sent messengers ahead to his brother Esau with words of greeting and friendship. The messengers returned with the report that Esau was on his way toward Jacob with four hundred men. Jacob was frightened and divided his people into two groups, so that if Esau attacked, at least one group might escape.

And Jacob sent his servants to meet Esau with rich presents—cows, camels, sheep, and oxen.

When the two brothers met, Jacob was overjoyed to behold Esau. Esau accepted the gifts and the two parted, united in brotherly love.

And Jacob came home to Canaan with his family and his possessions. And his father Isaac died at the age of one hundred and eighty years.

Genesis 32:4—36:43

VAYESHEV
וישב

Jacob had twelve sons and one daughter, and of his sons he loved Joseph best. When Joseph was seventeen, Jacob had a coat of many colors made for him. For this his brothers disliked him and their dislike turned to hatred when Joseph dreamed that he would one day rule over them.

Once, when his brothers had not returned with their father's flocks, Jacob sent Joseph to see if all was well. When the brothers saw Joseph approaching, they said: "Let us kill him and throw him into a pit."

However, at the insistence of Reuben, the eldest brother, they did not kill Joseph, but threw him into an empty pit alive.

They sat down to eat. A caravan of Ishmaelites came into view and the brothers thought of selling Joseph to the Ishmaelites. Meantime, a band of roving Midianites passed by. They lifted Joseph from the pit and sold him to the Ishmaelite caravan for twenty silver pieces. Thus was Joseph brought to Egypt.

When the brothers saw Joseph was missing, they were frightened. They dipped Joseph's coat of many colors into goat's blood and brought it to Jacob, who cried out: "Alas! A wild beast must have attacked my son!"

Nor would he be comforted.

Genesis 37:1—40:23

MIKETZ

מִקֵּץ

Joseph had been in prison for two full years when he was called out to explain Pharaoh's dreams.

Pharaoh had dreamed of seven fat cows being swallowed by seven lean cows, and of seven fat stalks of grain swallowed by seven lean ones. Joseph explained that seven years of plenty would be followed by seven years of hunger. Joseph then suggested that Pharaoh appoint a wise man to store away food during the good years ahead.

Pharaoh was pleased with this plan and appointed Joseph ruler over all his people.

Joseph was thirty years old when he became Pharaoh's prime minister. He managed well and when the famine came, people from every country thronged to Egypt to buy food, and among them were Joseph's own brothers. He recognized them at once, but they did not know him, and he ordered them to bring their youngest brother Benjamin on their next journey to Egypt.

This they did, and Joseph had a silver goblet secretly placed in Benjamin's grain sack. "The man who has stolen my goblet," said Joseph, "will be my slave!" When the goblet was discovered, Joseph insisted that Benjamin remain with him as his servant.

Genesis 41:1—44:17

VAYIGASH
ויגש

The other brothers were overcome with fear and sorrow when Joseph insisted that Benjamin remain in Egypt, for Benjamin was Jacob's youngest son, all that was left him of a beloved wife. Joseph was moved to pity and he ordered the court cleared, whereupon he revealed himself to his brothers.

"I am Joseph your brother, whom you sold into Egypt," he said. "Do not be ashamed, for God sent me before you to preserve life."

Then Joseph invited his brothers to come to live in Egypt and to bring their father there. When the brothers returned to Canaan and told Jacob that Joseph was alive and well, and that he was ruler over Egypt, Jacob wept with joy.

"Let us go, my sons, to the land of Egypt," he cried. "Joseph my son is yet alive; I will go and see him before I die."

Next morning Jacob set out from Beersheba. His sons took Jacob their father, their wives, and their little ones, in the wagons which Pharaoh had sent to carry them. And Jacob and all his family came to Egypt and settled there. Pharaoh was good to them and the Children of Israel were happy in his land.

Genesis 44:18—47:27

VAYEHI
ויחי

Jacob was one hundred and forty-seven years old and he felt his end was near. He had lived for seventeen happy years in Egypt. Now he called Joseph to him, and Joseph's two sons, Ephraim and Manasseh.

"My son," he said to Joseph, "swear to me that when I die, you will not bury me here in Egypt, but that you will carry me to Canaan, the land of my fathers, and bury me in the cave where they lie."

Joseph wept and took an oath to do his father's bidding. Then Jacob blessed Joseph by blessing Ephraim and Manasseh. "For I consider your sons as my own, and they will share with your brothers in the blessing of our people."

Now Jacob called for his other sons. "Gather round," he said, "and receive your blessings." And he gave a special blessing to each of them.

When Jacob died, Joseph and his brothers fulfilled his wish. They bore him to the land of Canaan and buried him in the Cave of Machpelah. Afterward, Joseph and his brothers returned to Egypt.

Joseph lived for one hundred and ten years. Before he died, Joseph said to his people: "God will surely remember you and bring you to the land which He promised to Abraham, Isaac, and Jacob."

Genesis 47:28—50:26

שמות

EXODUS

Exodus tells us about the hardships of the Israelites in Egypt and their escape from slavery under the guidance of Moses. Exodus also describes how the Jewish people received the Ten Commandments at Mount Sinai. It pictures the first Passover. Step by step, it details the building of the Sanctuary. The Hebrew name for Exodus is *Shemot* (Names) because it begins with a list of the names of Israel's sons in Egypt.

SHEMOT
שְׁמוֹת

Joseph and his brothers had lived peacefully in Egypt. At last they and all their generation died. A new Pharaoh arose and said: "Behold, the Israelites are too numerous. They have too much power in our kingdom!"

And Pharaoh ordered all male Israelites to be killed at birth. Now Amram and Jochebed, of the Tribe of Levi, had a baby son, and they hid him in a box at the edge of the Nile. There he was found by Pharaoh's daughter, who called him Moses ("the one drawn out") and raised him in the palace.

When Moses grew up, he saw an Egyptian taskmaster beating an Israelite slave. He looked around and did not see any other person. He struck down the Egyptian and hid his body in the sand. When Pharaoh heard of the Egyptian's death, he sought to have Moses put to death, but Moses escaped from Pharaoh to the land of Midian. There he tended the flocks of Jethro. Later Jethro gave Moses his daughter, Zipporah, to be his wife.

While tending his flocks in the desert of Sinai, Moses saw a burning thornbush. From the bush, which burned but was not destroyed, Moses heard the voice of God. The Lord said to Moses: "Go to Pharaoh and tell him to free Israel from slavery!"

Exodus 1:1—6:1

VA-EYRA
וארא

God spoke to Moses, saying: "Tell the Israelites that I will bring them out of Egypt and free them from slavery. And request of Pharaoh that he allow the Children of Israel to go out of his land."

When Pharaoh heard this, he grew more spiteful and mean than ever. He forbade his taskmasters to provide straw to the people to make bricks. Instead they had to hunt for the straw themselves. But the number of bricks they had to produce remained the same.

The leaders of Israel complained bitterly to Moses. Their lot was getting harder. The Lord ordered Moses and Aaron to go before Pharaoh a second time.

Aaron cast his rod before Pharaoh and it turned into a snake. Pharaoh's magicians did the same, but Aaron's rod swallowed all of theirs.

Nevertheless, Pharaoh refused to yield.

So the Lord sent ten plagues upon Egypt. The first plague turned all the waters of Egypt to blood. The fish died in the Nile and there was no drinking water in the land.

Still Pharaoh's heart remained hard. Then came frogs, lice, flies, and cattle-illness, boils, blisters, and hail.

But Pharaoh refused to free the Children of Israel.

Exodus 6:2—9:35

BO

בא

When the Lord saw that Pharaoh's heart was still hardened, He sent a plague of locusts followed by one of pitch blackness which darkened Egypt for three days.

Then God sent the last and most awful plague of all. That night, every first-born of every Egyptian family died.

Only the homes of the Israelites were untouched, for Moses had instructed the people to mark their doorposts with the blood of a lamb.

Terrified, Pharaoh summoned Moses and Aaron.

"Leave Egypt!" he cried. "Worship your Lord, as you have requested. Take your flocks and your herds, and go!"

Thus did the Children of Israel finally leave the land of bondage. They had no time to allow the bread they were baking to rise. They took the unleavened dough with them.

And Moses said: "When the Lord shall bring you to a land flowing with milk and honey, then must you observe the feast of Passover during this month; for seven days shall you eat unleavened bread, or matzot. And when your children ask, 'What do you mean by this service?' you shall answer, 'It is the Passover-service to the Lord, for He passed over the houses of the Israelites when He struck down the Egyptians."

Exodus 10:1—13:16

BESHALAH
בשלח

When the Israelites left Egypt, Pharaoh changed his mind and pursued them with his armies. The Children of Israel were frightened, but Moses said: "Do not be afraid. God will fight for you."

And Moses stretched his hand out over the Red Sea, as the Lord had instructed him. The waters parted and God provided a path, and the waters formed a wall on each side.

Pharaoh tried to follow the Israelites, but the waters returned and drowned all the Egyptians. That day did Moses and the Israelites sing a song of praise to God, saying:

"I will sing to God
He is my strength
For He has saved me."

When the Israelites had journeyed a while into the desert, and all their food was gone, they grew frightened again.

"Have you brought us here to die of hunger and of thirst?" they asked Moses and Aaron.

Again the Lord heard their complaint and He said to Moses: "Tell the Israelites that I will send food from heaven and water from the rocks; they will have plenty to eat and to drink."

The Children of Israel called this food manna, and they ate it and were strengthened.

Exodus 13:17—17:16

JETHRO
יתרו

In the desert, Moses was joined by his father-in-law, Jethro, who suggested that Moses appoint captains to help the people in their problems. Thus was Moses' heavy burden relieved.

In the third month after the Israelites had left Egypt, they camped at the foot of Mount Sinai. Moses ascended the mountain and there he listened to the voice of God.

"Tell the Israelites that if they obey Me, they will be a holy nation," said the Lord.

Moses proclaimed the words of the Lord to the Israelites.

All together, they said: "We will do all that the Lord asks."

For three days they waited. On the third day, amidst thunder and lightning, Moses once again ascended Mount Sinai. In fear and silence, the Israelites heard the Lord give Moses the ten great commandments by which they were to live.

God spoke, saying: "I am the Lord your God. You shall have no other gods before Me. Do not use the name of your Lord carelessly. Keep holy the Sabbath Day. Honor your father and mother. Do not kill. Do not commit adultery. Do not steal. Do not accuse anyone falsely. Do not envy others."

And God gave Moses two stone tablets on which the Ten Commandments were written down.

Exodus 18:1—20:23

MISHPATIM
מִשְׁפָּטִים

When Moses ascended Mount Sinai he entered into the midst of a cloud. And he remained on Mount Sinai forty days and forty nights.

And the Lord gave Moses a set of rules and regulations by which Israel was to live and be holy. Among the rules of conduct transmitted through Moses to the Israelites were the following:

—If a man kills another accidentally, he is to be given a place to hide from angry relatives. But if he strikes another on purpose and he dies, the murderer must be put to death.

—Should a man curse his father or his mother, he is to be put to death.

—Should an Israelite lend money to another of his people who is poor, then the lender may charge no interest.

—For six years the Israelites are to sow their land and gather in the harvest, but on the seventh year the land must rest and not be planted, so that the poor people may gather what is left in the fields.

—The festivals of Passover, Shavuot, and Sukkot are to be observed each year, so that the Israelites may remember what the Lord did for them.

Thus did the laws set down in this sidra emphasize the justice that prevails in Judaism.

Exodus 21:1—24:18

TERUMAH
תרומה

While Moses was on Mount Sinai, the Lord commanded him to tell the Children of Israel to build a Tabernacle, so that God could dwell among them.

In the Tabernacle, or Mishkan, there was to be a Holy Ark. God said: "Make the Ark of acacia wood. Inside the Ark you will put the Laws which I will give you. Make a cover of pure gold for the Ark."

Moses was also instructed to place inside the Tabernacle a table of acacia wood, bearing twelve hallot — the "showbread" — equal in number to the Twelve Tribes of Israel.

The contents of the Mishkan also included a Menorah of pure gold. God said: "Make the Mishkan with ten curtains of fine twined linen, and blue, purple, and scarlet. Another curtain made the same way is to be hung on four columns of acacia wood overlaid with gold, and resting on four posts of silver.

"And you shall place the Ark of the Law in the space where the Curtain divides the Holy Place from the Holy of Holies."

Finally, there was to be a square Altar fitted with rings and poles, so that it could be carried. Surrounding all these holy objects there was to be a courtyard about 150 feet long and 75 feet wide, enclosed by curtains of fine linen.

Exodus 25:1—27:19

TETZAVEH

תצוה

And God ordained that the Children of Israel maintain an eternal light for the sanctuary. Thus did the Lord command Moses:

"You shall instruct the Children of Israel to bring you pure olive oil to be used for a lamp to burn continuously. And Aaron and his sons shall set up this lamp—the Ner Tamid—in the Tabernacle."

The Eternal Light was to burn evening and morning. Further, God commanded Moses to appoint his brother Aaron and his sons to serve as priests. They were to wear holy garments when they performed their holy duties.

These were among the garments to be made: a breastplate, a robe, an ephod (upper garment), a tunic, a headdress, and a sash. All were to be made of gold, blue, purple, and scarlet thread and fine linen.

The names of the tribes of Israel were to be engraved on two onyx stones and placed in settings of gold on the shoulder straps of the ephod. And in the breastplate were to be set twelve precious stones bearing the names of the Tribes.

In this manner were the Israelites taught that although every individual must serve God, a special group of devoted servants must be at the forefront of spiritual leadership.

Exodus 27:20—30:10

KI TISSA

כי תשא

All these things and many more the Lord said to Moses on Mount Sinai. And when the people saw how long Moses remained on Mount Sinai, they said to Aaron:

"Make us a god that we can see, for we do not know what has happened to Moses."

Aaron could not persuade the people that they were wrong, so he told them to bring all their golden jewelry. He melted the gold and made of it a calf.

The next morning, the people of Israel held a festival in honor of the golden calf. The Lord saw what was happening and He ordered Moses to return to the people. Moses descended, bearing the Ten Commandments.

When Moses beheld his people worshipping a golden calf, he grew angry and dashed the Two Tablets to the ground. Then he destroyed the golden calf.

When the people realized how they had sinned, they mourned deeply and pleaded with Moses to return to the mountain.

Once again Moses ascended Mt. Sinai, and the Lord gave him another set of Tablets. When Moses came down, his face shone with the glory of God. And the Children of Israel were awed by the rays of brilliant light which came from his face and they promised never to worship idols again.

Exodus 30:11—34:35

VAYAKHEL

ויקהל

Moses called together all the Children of Israel and said to them: "These are God's commandments to you.

"Six days a week may you work, but on the seventh day you shall observe a Shabbat, a day of rest, holy to God."

And Moses asked everyone who wanted to do so with his whole heart to give a special contribution toward the building of the Tabernacle. They could give gold, silver, or brass; fine linen, goatskins, acacia wood, or oil for lighting the Eternal Light.

Moses also asked skilled workmen to step forward to help construct the Tabernacle.

Bezalel and Oholiab, both highly skilled craftsmen, led the workers who built the Tabernacle. And the people were so generous that they continued to bring contributions every morning. At last the workmen told Moses that no more materials were needed for the work.

So Moses announced to the entire encampment that contributions were to be halted, and that no man or woman was to bring any further contribution.

And the people listened and obeyed, happy that more than enough was already on hand for the work commanded by God.

Exodus 35:1—38:20

PEKUDAY

פקודי

In time, all the work on the Tabernacle was finished, and the Israelites did as the Lord had commanded Moses. Each of the Israelites brought a gift with which to make the Lord's Ark and Tabernacle beautiful. Bezalel and Oholiab, the two chief craftsmen, supervised the work.

For the Lord had said: "On the first day of the first month shall you erect the Tent of Meeting. And you shall put therein the Holy Ark, and the table and the showbread, and the candlestick. And you shall set the golden altar before the Ark."

Now when Moses saw that the Children of Israel did all that God had commanded, he blessed them and caused the Tent of Meeting to be set up.

Then a cloud covered the Tent of Meeting, and the glory of the Lord filled the Tabernacle. The Israelites prepared themselves to march. Whenever the cloud was raised above the Tabernacle, the Israelites would march ahead, throughout all their journeys, but whenever the cloud was not raised, they would not move until it was lifted.

The cloud of the Lord covered the Tabernacle by day, and at night there was a fire in the cloud, in sight of all the house of Israel, throughout all their journeys.

Exodus 38:21—40:38

ויקרא

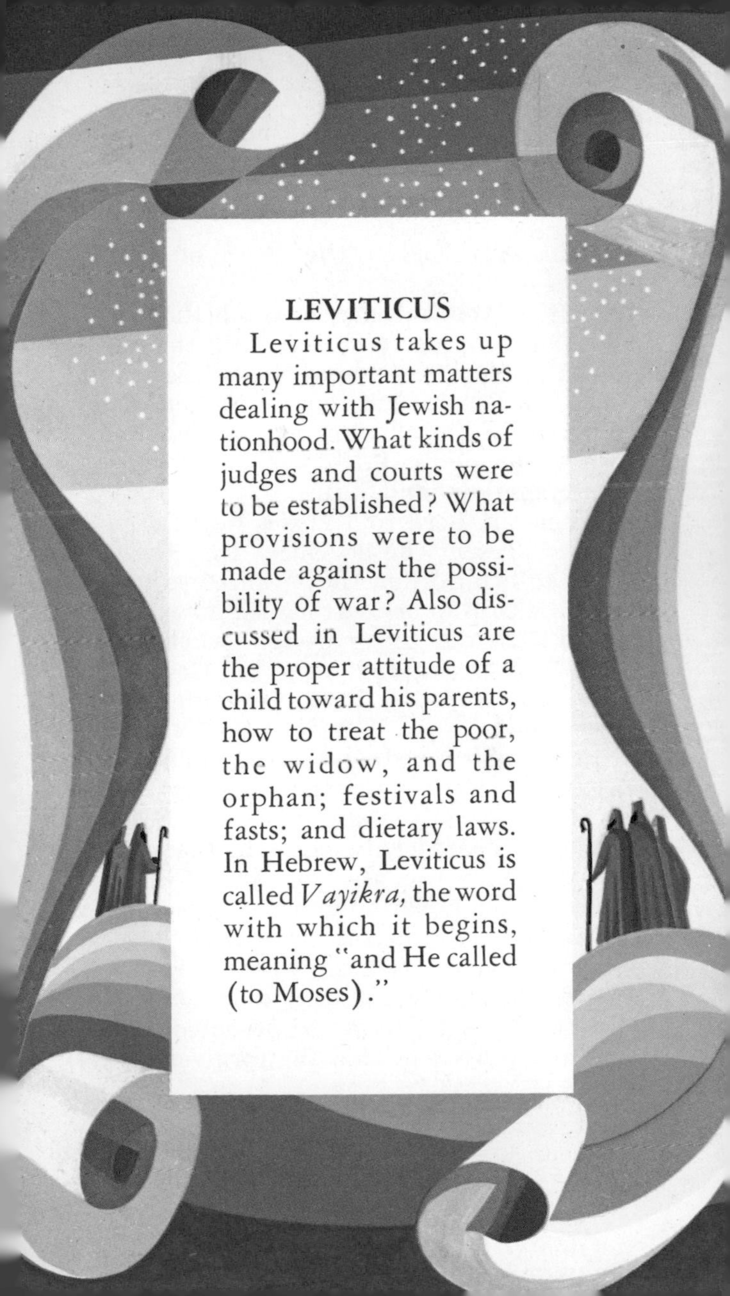

LEVITICUS

Leviticus takes up many important matters dealing with Jewish nationhood. What kinds of judges and courts were to be established? What provisions were to be made against the possibility of war? Also discussed in Leviticus are the proper attitude of a child toward his parents, how to treat the poor, the widow, and the orphan; festivals and fasts; and dietary laws. In Hebrew, Leviticus is called *Vayikra,* the word with which it begins, meaning "and He called (to Moses)."

VAYIKRA

ויקרא

This sidra opens the third of the Five Books of Moses.

Out of the Tabernacle came the voice of the Lord, saying to Moses, "Tell the children of Israel that they may bring these offerings unto Me: An Olah, or burnt offering; a Minhah, or meal offering; a Shlamim, or peace offering; a Hattat, or sin offering; and an Asham, or guilt offering."

Then the Lord told Moses how the priests should present the sacrifices that the people were to bring when they wanted to make an offering to Him or to atone for a wrongdoing.

An Olah was to be brought when a person felt sorry for having forgotten God. It could be taken from the herd, from the flock, or from fowl.

A Minhah was to be made when someone wished to offer thanks and show his gratitude to God. He could make it of flour, wheat, or barley, prepared with oil or incense.

A Shlamim was another kind of thanks-offering, brought for a happy occasion in family or nation, and taken from herd or flock.

A Hattat or Asham was to be brought when, through error, a person committed a forbidden deed. The priest accepted the offering and prayed to God for forgiveness.

Leviticus 1:1—5:26

TZAV

צו

This sidra continues to describe the laws of sacrifice for the individual, for the congregation, and for the priests. The previous sidra, Vayikra, spoke to the Children of Israel and concerned the whole people. This sidra was meant to be a ritual guide-book for the priests.

All the Israelites were assembled before the Tabernacle, when Moses made it holy and anointed Aaron as High Priest.

This is how Moses made Aaron the High Priest. He washed Aaron and his sons, put the tunic on Aaron, tied the sash around his waist, dressed him in the robe and breastplate in which he had placed the holy Urim and Tummim. Then he set the golden crown upon his head. Next, Moses sprinkled some of the anointing oil upon the head of Aaron.

Then he said to Aaron and his sons: "For seven days you must not leave the Tabernacle. In this time, you will make yourself holy for service to God."

On the eighth day, Moses summoned Aaron and his sons and said: "Offer a sacrifice upon the Altar before God." Aaron did so. Then Moses and Aaron blessed the Children of Israel.

Leviticus 6:1—8:36

SHEMINI
שְׁמִינִי

Moses called Aaron and his sons and the elders of Israel and gave them detailed instructions concerning the living things which they might eat.

Only animals which had parted hoofs and chewed their cud might be eaten. But an animal which had only parted hoofs or which only chewed its cud could not be eaten. Thus the camel and the rabbit were forbidden, for they chewed their cud but had no parted hoof. Nor was the pig clean food, for while it had a parted hoof it did not chew its cud.

Fish which had fins and scales could be eaten.

Birds of prey—those which eat other living things—like the vulture, eagle, and hawk; and all wild birds, like the ostrich, raven, bat, and stork, were to be considered unclean.

Nor could crawling insects be eaten. All winged things that go upon all four were forbidden. Unclean, too, were the weasel, the mouse, the lizard, the crocodile, and the chameleon.

The Israelites were also forbidden to eat blood of any kind.

Since the daily diet affects a man's whole being, the kinds of food a Jew is permitted to eat holds an important place in the laws of holiness.

Leviticus 9:1—11:47

TAZRIA
תזריע

Over and over again, the Israelites were told that they were to be a holy people. They were to avoid everything that displeased God and were to lead pure and upright lives. "You shall be holy," they were told, "for I the Lord your God am holy."

Since a person who was not clean according to the laws of the Torah was not permitted to enter the Tabernacle, special laws were laid down on the subject of health and cleanliness.

In ancient times, a dread and well-known disease was leprosy, and the Torah painstakingly describes the manner in which this disease could be detected and how it was to be treated.

"The priest must examine the diseased spot. If it is leprosy, the man is unclean. The priest shall separate the diseased man for seven days. Then the priest will examine the man again. If the spot is disappearing, then the priest shall pronounce him clean. But if it has spread, then must the leprous man tear his clothes, wear his hair loose, live away from the camp, and warn people not to touch him."

Leviticus 12:1—13:59

METZORA
מצורע

In this sidra, the Torah continues to discuss laws of religious purity.

God said to Moses: "When a leper is cured of his illness, he must be pronounced healed by a priest. Let him be brought to the priest who will be waiting outside the camp. The priest will examine him to see if the disease of leprosy is indeed healed.

"When the priest shall say the man is healed, then let him wash his clothes, shave off his hair and bathe himself in water. After eight days, let him offer sacrifices."

Thus was the leper purified.

And thus did the Torah take notice of a disease which in ancient days was dread and all-too-widespread. Leprosy was fearful not only because of what it did to the person who unfortunately was afflicted with it, but also because of the terrible speed with which it could spread.

Other nations were much harsher in their attitude towards lepers in their midst. The Israelites, obeying the laws of God as expressed in the Torah, tried to help the leper and to treat him as humanely as possible.

Leviticus 14:1—15:33

AHAREY MOT
אחרי מות

God commanded Moses to set aside the tenth day of the seventh month of Tishri as a Day of Atonement for the Israelites.

"On this day," said the Lord, "shall atonement be made for you, to cleanse you for your sins."

The people were to refrain from all pleasures and all work, and they were to fast the whole day. The High Priest was to wear special garments, "the holy linen garments," and offer sacrifices to the Lord to atone for himself and all the Children of Israel because of the sins they had done during the year.

Only on this one day of the entire year was the High Priest permitted to come close to the Holy Ark. And only on this day was he to wear not his golden garments but white linen, symbol of purity and humility. On his appearance at the conclusion of the service, he was greeted with rejoicing by the people, confident that their sins had been forgiven.

It is interesting to note that the word atonement is made up of two words—"at" and "one." On this day of "at-one-ment" Jews from time immemorial have sought to be "at one"—in harmony with God.

Leviticus 16:1—18:30

KEDOSHIM
קדֹשים

The Lord spoke to Moses, saying: "Tell the Children of Israel to be holy, for I the Lord your God am holy.

"Revere your mother and your father, every one of you, for I the Lord your God, am holy.

"You shall not steal; you shall not cheat; you shall not tell a lie to one another. You shall not take a false oath in My name. You shall not deceive your neighbor, nor rob him.

"You shall not curse a deaf man, nor cause a blind person to stumble. Fear your God: I am the Lord.

"If a stranger comes to your land to stay, treat him well; think of him as one of yourselves, as if he were a native.

"You shall love your neighbor as you love yourself; I am the Lord.

"You shall rise up before a man with white hair, and honor the person of an old man, standing in awe of your God: I am the Lord.

"If you will keep My laws, then will you inherit the land, for I will give it to you to keep it, a land flowing with milk and honey."

Thus did God caution the Israelites to walk in His ways and in this fashion did they learn at an early stage in their nationhood that reverence for God equals respect for man.

Leviticus 19:1—20:27

EMOR
אמר

Because the Israelites promised to obey God's laws, He vowed to give them a land flowing with milk and honey. Among the things which set them apart were their festivals. God repeated the laws of festivals to Moses and through him to all the people of Israel.

The Lord said: "The seventh day of each week shall be a Shabbat, a day of holy rest, and no work shall be done in your homes.

"At sunset of the fourteenth day of the first month, let the Passover begin. For seven days shall you eat matzot.

"And when you gather in the harvest, you shall bring the first fruits to the priest. And you shall count seven full weeks after that and proclaim a holy gathering which shall be known as the Feast of Weeks—Shavuot.

"The first day of the seventh month shall be Rosh Hashanah—the New Year—on which you shall blow the shofar. The tenth day of the seventh month shall be Yom Kippur—the Day of Atonement.

"On the fifteenth day of the seventh month, let the Feast of Tabernacles, Sukkot, begin. You shall live in booths for seven days so that you and your children may remember that you lived in booths when I brought you out of the land of Egypt. I am your God."

Leviticus 21:1—24:23

BEHAR

בהר

The Israelites were a farming nation. In order to keep the land from falling into the hands of a few people, making slaves of many, Moses ordained two basic laws.

One was the law of Shemitah, or the Sabbatical Year, a year of rest for the land to prevent it from being worn out. This came every seventh year, and whatever grew during that year was free to all.

The other was the law of Yovel, or the Jubilee Year, which came each fiftieth year. In that year, every Israelite slave was set free, and all the land which had been sold was to be restored to the hands of the original owner or to his heirs.

The Lord gave these laws to Moses on Mount Sinai, saying: "For six years shall you sow your field and gather your crops, but the seventh year shall be a year of rest for the land.

"You shall count forty-nine years. Then, on Yom Kippur, the shofar shall be blown, and you shall declare the fiftieth year holy.

"Then you shall proclaim liberty throughout the land to all the inhabitants thereof."

With these words did the Lord command the Israelites to respect the rights and the privileges of their fellow men.

Leviticus 25:1—26:2

BEHUKOTAI

בחקתי

This sidra brings to a close the third of the Five Books of Moses—the Book of Leviticus. In it, the Children of Israel are told that if they obey God's laws they will prosper and be well. On the other hand, should they stray from the path of righteousness, disorder and unhappiness would follow.

Over and again the Lord reminded His people of basic rules. "Make no idols for yourselves; nor shall you set up statues to bow down to. For I am the Lord your God.

"If you live by My laws, I will send the rains at the right time, and the land shall yield its harvests and the trees their fruits.

"I will be good to you and make you fruitful and multiply you. For I brought you out of Egypt and broke your chains of slavery and made you free men.

"But if you will not listen to Me, you will live in confusion and fear. Your enemies will eat your harvest, and they will conquer you. You will be scattered among the nations.

"Not until you observe My laws again will I remember My promise to your ancestors. Only then will I be good to you."

These were the commandments which the Lord commanded Moses for the Children of Israel on Mount Sinai.

Leviticus 26:3—27:34

עצרת

NUMBERS

Numbers tells what happened to the Israelites from the time they left Mount Sinai until they reached the borders of Canaan. The trials of the pioneers are described and the problems of their new-found freedom are analyzed. The Hebrew name for Numbers is *Bemidbar,* from its first important word, meaning "in the wilderness." The name "Numbers" refers to the numbering, or census, of the Israelites as they began their journey toward the Promised Land.

BEMIDBAR
במדבר

This sidra opens the fourth of the Five Books of Moses. Numbers describes the wanderings of the Israelites in the desert and shows how God watched over them at all times. It also deals with rules and regulations for the Tabernacle and the family.

In the sidra of Bemidbar, we learn how Moses was told to gather all the people, one month after the Tabernacle was built, and to take the first census of Israel.

Each tribe was registered, family by family, and every able-bodied man of twenty years and over, fit for military service, was counted, just as God had ordered. The total was 603,550.

The Levites were placed in charge of the Tabernacle. God then ordered Moses to place the Israelites' tents around the Tabernacle. Each tent was to have a banner, showing the tribe to which it belonged. Then the Levites were counted, and there were 22,000 Levites.

After that the first-born males were counted, and there were 22,273.

Then the Lord said to Moses: "Redeem the 273 first-born males that exceed in number all the Levites. Let each give five shekels apiece to Aaron and his sons." And Moses received the shekels and turned them over to Aaron and his sons. And God's will was done.

Numbers 1:1—4:20

NASSO
נשׂא

During the long years of wandering in the desert, Moses used all his patience and wisdom to mold the Israelites into a powerful, united people. He strengthened them morally and spiritually by repeating the laws of cleanliness without which a young nation might fall into decay and sickness.

"Tell the Israelites," said the Lord, "that they must remove from their camp those who suffer from leprosy and those who have become unclean by touching a dead body. They must not make the camp unclean for My spirit is among them.

"Remember this: when a man or a woman does a wrong against a fellow man it shall be considered a sin against the Lord. They shall confess their sin and return to the owner what they have taken, adding to it a fifth of what it is worth."

The Lord did not only admonish the Children of Israel; He also demonstrated His love for them by blessing them. The Lord said to Moses: "Tell Aaron and his sons, 'With these words shall you bless the Israelites: May the Lord bless you and keep you! May the Lord make His face shine upon you and be gracious unto you! May the Lord lift up His countenance upon you and give you peace!' "

These words have comprised the Priestly Benediction from those days unto our own.

Numbers 4:21—7:89

BEHAALOTEKHA
בהעלתך

God commanded Moses to organize the tribes in their marching order. The Ark of the Covenant was carried at the head of the marching hosts, a symbol of God's presence and protection.

Two silver trumpets were used for calling the people together and for starting the journey. God said:

"When both trumpets are blown, the entire congregation shall gather around you, but when one trumpet is blown only the chiefs shall gather around you.

"The sons of Aaron, the priests, shall be the only ones to blow the trumpets. You shall blow your trumpets when you make your offerings at your festivals, and on Rosh Hodesh, the first day of the month."

In the second year, on the twentieth day of the second month, the cloud over the Tabernacle was lifted, and the Israelites traveled from the wilderness of Sinai.

The Levites bore the Ark. When they started, Moses said a prayer: "Rise up O Lord and let Your enemies be scattered . . ." And when they brought the Ark to rest, Moses would say: "Return, O Lord, unto the ten thousands of the families of Israel."

To this day the prayers of Moses are chanted at the opening and closing of the Ark, whenever the Torah is read.

Numbers 8:1—12:16

SHELAH

שלח

God said to Moses: "Send one man from each of the Twelve Tribes to look over the Land of Canaan secretly."

The scouts sent by Moses came to the valley of Eshkol and cut down a branch with one cluster of grapes, which they bore upon a pole between two men. They also took back pomegranates and figs.

And this was their report: "The land flows with milk and honey. But its people are powerful; they live in fortresses, and there are among them giants who made us look like grasshoppers."

Only two of the scouts, Joshua and Caleb, were in favor of moving ahead at once to conquer the land. The Children of Israel were afraid.

"Let us go back to Egypt," they cried.

The Lord was very angry and said to Moses: "How long will they not believe in Me, despite the wonders I have shown them?"

The Lord forgave the stubborn Children of Israel. However, because they showed lack of faith in Him, He told them that only their children would reach the Promised Land.

This event showed that the Israelites were not ready to be a free nation. During thirty-eight years of wandering, a new generation was to grow up. This generation would be ready to conquer the Promised Land.

Numbers 13:1—15:41

KORAH

קרח

Korah, with Dathan and Aviram, and 250 other Israelites, revolted against Moses and Aaron.

"We are all holy!" they cried. "Why do you make yourselves greater than the rest of us?"

Moses replied: "You are Levites and do God's holy work in the Tabernacle. Do you wish to be priests, too?"

Moses ordered Korah, Dathan, Aviram, and their followers to bring offerings to God together with Aaron on the following day. As they stood there, ceremonial fire-pans in hand, Moses said to the people: "If these men die an unnatural death, then you shall know that they have offended the Lord."

As Moses finished speaking, the ground split and swallowed up Korah, his followers, and their households. They vanished from the community.

But the people still murmured. Then God told Moses to take a rod from the leader of each tribe, and write the name of each on his rod, and Aaron's name on the rod of Levi. Moses placed these in the Tent of Meeting. By the next day, the rod of Aaron had blossomed and produced almonds.

And Aaron's rod was kept in front of the Ark as a sign for rebellious men.

Numbers 16:1—18:32

HUKKAT

חקת

Throughout their wanderings the Lord always helped the Israelites.

When they came to the desert of Zin, they found no water there. The people grumbled and said to Moses: "Have you brought us here to die? We cannot live without water."

The Lord said to Moses: "Take your rod and speak to the rock you see before you, and water will flow from the rock."

But Moses lifted his rod and struck the rock twice. Water flowed forth abundantly, and the Israelites' thirst was quenched. And the Lord said to Moses and Aaron: "Because you smote the rock instead of speaking to it, therefore will you not lead the Israelites into the Promised Land."

Now the Israelites came to Mount Hor, and the Lord said: "The time has come for Aaron to die. Take Aaron and his son Eleazar up to Mount Hor. Strip Aaron of his robes and put them on Eleazar; and Aaron shall die there."

Moses did as the Lord told him. Aaron died and the people mourned him for thirty days.

The Israelites traveled northward. They vanquished the Amorites and defeated Og, king of Bashan, and all his army. And the Children of Israel journeyed to the plains of Moab beyond the Jordan at Jericho.

Numbers 19:1—22:1

BALAK

בלק

The Israelites now entered upon the last stage of their journey to the Promised Land.

And Balak, king of Moab, saw what had happened to the Amorites and he was very frightened. He sent messengers to Balaam, the great magician of the city of Pethor, saying: "The Israelites have reached my borders. Please come and curse this people for me."

Balaam agreed. He set out on his donkey. And the Lord sent a shining angel to block his path.

Three times the donkey turned aside and three times Balaam beat her cruelly.

Suddenly the creature spoke: "Why do you beat me, master?"

Then God opened Balaam's eyes and he beheld the angel. And Balaam was humbled and, instead of cursing the Israelites, he blessed them, saying:

> "How goodly are your tents, O Jacob,
> Your dwelling places, O Israel.
> As valleys stretched out
> As gardens by the river-side.
> Blessed be every one who blesses you,
> And cursed be everyone who curses you."

And thus did a renowned heathen prophet prophesy that Israel was destined to become a great and glorious nation.

Numbers 22:2-25:9

PINHAS
פינחס

Moses was old; his great work had drawn to a close. Now he concerned himself about Israel's future leader. The people were eager to take possession of the Promised Land, and they needed young but experienced leadership.

The Lord said to Moses: "Ascend this mountain and see the land which I have given the Israelites. When you have seen it, you also will be gathered to your people, as your brother Aaron was."

Moses said: "Let the Lord appoint a leader over the people, so that they may not be like sheep that have no shepherd."

And the Lord answered: "Take Joshua, the son of Nun, for he is a man of wisdom, courage, and holiness. Bring him before Eleazar, the priest, and all the congregation of Israel. Transfer your leadership to him by laying your hand upon him, in their presence, so that they may know he is now their leader."

Moses did as the Lord commanded him.

He placed Joshua before Eleazar, the priest, and before all the people. And he laid his hand on Joshua and prepared him to assume the mantle of leadership.

Numbers 25:10—30:1

MATTOT
מטּוֹת

The tribe of Reuben and the tribe of Gad had a great number of cattle, and they wanted to stay in the land east of the Jordan, for it was good for cattle feeding.

But Moses said: "Shall the other tribes go to war while you stay here?"

They replied: "We will march with the Israelites and will not return here until we have brought them to their land, and each one has received his share. We ourselves will not ask for any share of their land on the other side of the Jordan because our share is here on the eastern side."

Then Moses commanded Eleazar, the priest, and Joshua, and the chiefs of the tribes: "If the tribes of Gad and Reuben will cross the Jordan with you, armed and ready to fight for the Lord, and you conquer the land, then you shall give them the land east of the Jordan as their share.

"But if they will not cross it with you and join in the fight then they will have to give up the land east of the Jordan and fight for a share of the land of Canaan."

The tribes of Gad and Reuben repeated: "We will cross and fight with you."

Numbers 30:2—32:42

יהודה
זבולן
שמעון
גד
ראובן

MASSAY

מסעי

The final sidra of the Book of Numbers summarizes the route of the forty years of wandering.

It also describes the instructions given to the Israelites concerning the treatment of the conquered nations and the manner in which they were to divide the land of Canaan.

"Drive out all the people who live in the land of Canaan and destroy all their stone and metal idols," said the Lord. "Throw down their altars and places of worship.

"Then shall you occupy the land and live there. Draw lots and according to them divide the land among you, tribe by tribe. Give the greater share of the land to the larger tribes and the smaller share to the smaller tribes."

And Moses spoke to the Children of Israel, saying: "This is the land the Lord has given to the nine and one-half tribes. Share it by lot. As for the tribe of Reuben, the tribe of Gad, and half the tribe of Manasseh, these two and one-half tribes have received their share on the eastern side of the Jordan at Jericho."

These are the laws which the Lord gave through Moses unto the Children of Israel in the plains of Moab by the Jordan at Jericho.

Numbers 33:1—36:13

לערים

DEUTERONOMY

Deuteronomy reviews the history and the laws contained in the Books of Exodus, Leviticus, Numbers. It stresses the need for mankind to remember that God rules the entire world. The book closes with the poetic song and blessing of Moses just before the great leader died. The Hebrew name for Deuteronomy is *Devarim,* or "words," and comes from the first verse, which reads, "and these are the words which Moses spoke."

DEVARIM

דברים

The Fifth Book of Moses begins with Devarim—"the words." These are the words which Moses spoke to Israel. That is the theme of *Deuteronomy*: Moses' last addresses to his people.

He reviewed the history of their march through the wilderness, saying: "We traveled through the desert and you complained. God grew angry and said that none of this evil generation except Caleb and Joshua would ever see the Promised Land. Even I will not be allowed to see it.

"We marched for many days by way of the Red Sea, around Mount Seir. And then we went towards the prairies of Moab. We conquered the land of the Amorite kings east of the Jordan and we gave this territory to the tribe of Reuben, the tribe of Gad, and half the tribe of Manasseh.

"And I encouraged Joshua at that time, saying: 'Your eyes have seen all that the Lord your God has done to the enemies of Israel; so shall the Lord do unto all the kingdoms that attempt to conquer and oppress you. You shall not fear them; for the Lord your God, He it is Who fights for you.' "

Deuteronomy 1:1—3:22

VA-ETHANAN
ואתחנן

After Moses had reviewed the events that had taken place from the time the Israelites left Egypt to the moment they stood on the frontiers of Canaan, he urged the people to obey and carry out the Covenant between them and God.

Moses said: "Now, O Israel, hearken to the rules which I teach you, and obey them; for they will prove your wisdom and understanding in the eyes of the peoples.

"Tell your children and your children's children how you stood before the Lord at Mount Sinai, for the Lord made the Ten Commandments known to you on that day."

Moses then continued with the great declaration which we know as the Shema, the confession of belief in the unity of God.

"Hear, O Israel: the Lord our God, the Lord is One.

"And you shall love the Lord with all your heart and all your soul and all your might. And these words shall be upon your heart, and you shall teach them to your children. And you shall bind them for a sign upon your hand, and they shall be for frontlets between your eyes *(Tefillin)*. And you shall write them upon the doorposts of your house and upon your gates *(Mezuzah)*."

Deuteronomy 3:23—7:11

EKEV
עֵקֶב

In summarizing the laws, Moses stressed their inner spirit—God's love for Israel and the need of Israel's love for God. He reminded the Israelites of the close relationship which must always exist between them and the Almighty.

"And now, Israel," said Moses, "what does the Lord your God ask of you, but to reverence the Lord your God, to walk in His ways, to love Him, to worship Him with all your heart and all your soul; and to obey the rules and regulations which I command you this day.

"If you will always observe and practice all these commandments which I am giving you, to love the Lord your God, and to be loyal to Him, then the Lord your God will drive out all these nations before you and you shall conquer nations greater and mightier than you are yourselves; every place you pass through shall be yours, from the desert to Lebanon; from the Euphrates River to the Mediterranean Sea shall be your border. No one will be able to stand against you, for the Lord your God will put the fear of you in everyone's heart, as He has told you."

Deuteronomy 7:12—11:25

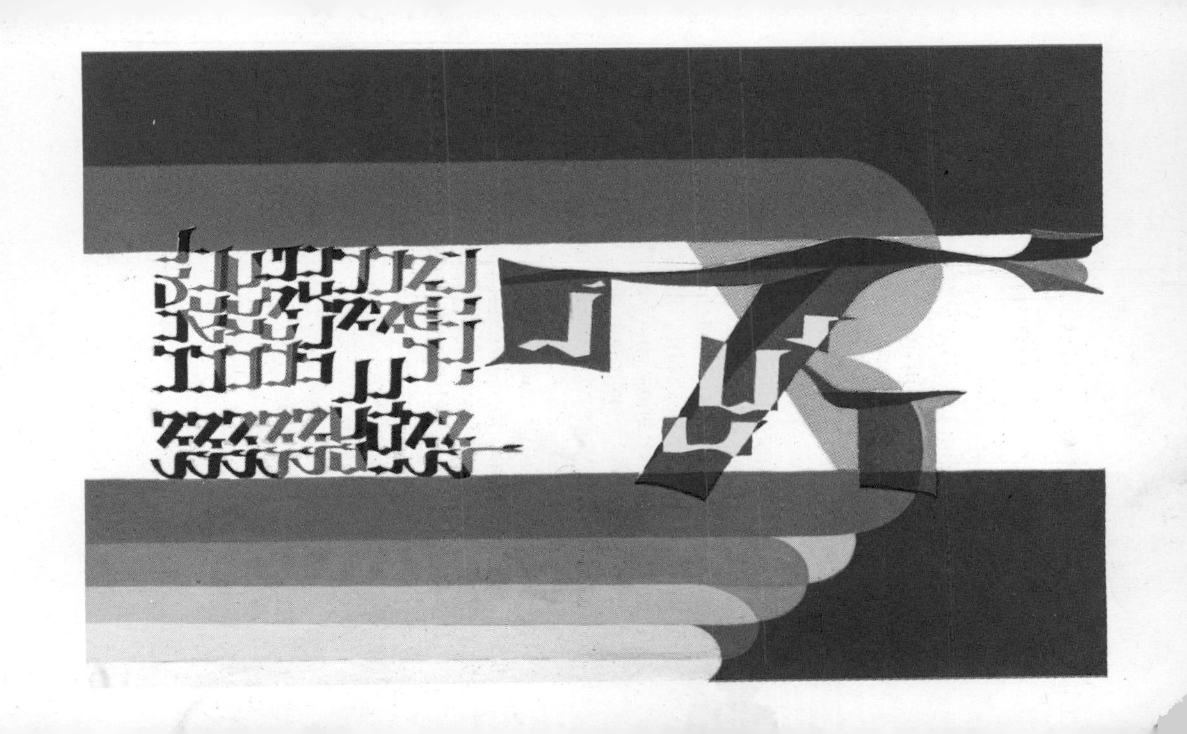

R'AY
ראה

Moses called together the Children of Israel. He repeated the laws by which they must live, and laid the foundation for the practice of *tzedakah* or righteousness, observed by our people to this day. He said to the priests and the Levites:

"After you have entered the Land of Canaan, arrange the Israelites by tribes facing each other on Mount Gerizim and Mount Ebal. There you will teach the rewards they will receive if they obey God's laws and the punishments if they disobey."

And Moses reminded the Israelites that they were always to take care of the poor among them.

"At the end of every three years," he said, "you shall contribute taxes for the poor—for the Levite (for he has no share in the land), for the stranger, the orphan, and the widow.

"After every seventh year, you shall free everyone from loans borrowed because of trouble in the family.

"For God has said: 'There will always be poor people among you; therefore, never refuse to help the poor and needy in your land.' "

Deuteronomy 11:26—16:17

SHOFETIM
שֹׁפְטִים

"Appoint judges and officers in each tribe, and let them judge the people righteously and fairly.

"Do not accept a bribe, for a bribe makes blind even a wise man.

"If a difficult case should arise, take it to the place chosen by the Lord your God; and the priests, the Levites, and the chief judge shall tell you of their decision; and you must carry out the judgment just as they tell you.

"When you come to the Promised Land and you wish to appoint a king over you, then choose one of your own people, and one whom the Lord your God shall approve. Let him not, however, gather military strength, nor shall he introduce idol-worship by taking many wives from foreign nations, nor shall he become rich at the expense of the people.

"When you besiege a city and conquer it, you shall not destroy the trees in it by wielding an axe against them. You may eat of their fruit, but do not cut them down. Only those trees which are not fruit-bearing may you cut down, so that you may build fortifications against invasion."

Thus did the Lord continue to create laws for Israel so that it might live as an honorable and upright nation.

Deuteronomy 16:18—21:9

KI TAYTZAY
כִּי תֵצֵא

Moses continued his oration, describing to the Israelites the humane laws which were to be observed with joyousness of spirit and sincerity of heart.

He said: "If you find a bird's nest in a tree or on the ground, with fledglings or eggs, and the mother bird sitting on them, you shall not take the mother bird with the little ones. First you shall let the mother bird go, and then you may take the young ones for yourself.

"Never cheat a hired worker whether he is one of your people or a stranger who lives in your land; you shall pay him every day when his day's work is done.

"Be especially truthful when a matter concerns a stranger, an orphan, or a widow. Remember that you were slaves in Egypt and the Lord your God freed you; therefore I give you this commandment.

"Do not use two sets of weights and measures; you must use perfect and exact ones, both for buying and selling, so that you may live long and happily in the land which the Lord your God is giving you.

"For all who deal falsely, all who live in ways that are not righteous, are hateful to the Lord your God."

Deuteronomy 21:10—25:19

KI TAVO

כִּי תָבוֹא

Moses said: "When you enter the land which God will give you and when you settle there, then shall you take the first fruit of your land and put it in a basket and bring it to your priest.

"He will take the basket and offer it to God. And you will be happy, you and the Levite and the stranger among you."

And the people understood that this was to be a symbol of thanksgiving to God, because He had rescued them from hardship and raised them to be a great nation.

Moses continued, saying: "If you will observe all the commandments of God, you will be showered with all of the blessings which I shall now pronounce.

> "You shall be blessed in the city and on the farm;
> You shall be blessed with many children;
> With fine harvests and cattle and sheep;
> You shall be blessed with food a-plenty;
> You shall be blessed when you return to your home and when you leave it."

But Moses warned the Children of Israel to remember that these blessings would be theirs only if they heeded God's word. He cautioned them to bear in mind that if they would not practice God's commandments, then would the blessings He had promised turn to bitter curses.

Deuteronomy 26:1—29:8

NITZAVIM
נִצָּבִים

At Mount Ebal and Mount Gerizim, Israel publicly entered into the Covenant made between their fathers and God. Moses taught them there the rewards and punishments of the Covenant. He reminded them:

"You are standing this day before the Lord your God—the heads of your tribes, your elders, your officers, all the men of Israel, together with your children, wives, and the strangers among you; so that He may establish you this day as His own people, and that he may be to you a God, as He promised you and as He swore to your fathers, Abraham, Isaac, and Jacob."

And Moses, the great Prophet, foresaw the days and events to come:

"I have set before you this day life and good, and death and evil. If you love the Lord your God, then you shall live and prosper.

"Choose life, therefore, that you and your children may live, by loving the Lord and obeying His commandments.

"This commandment is not too hard for you, nor is it far off. It is not in heaven nor beyond the sea. The word is very near you, in your mouth, and in your heart, so that you may do it."

Deuteronomy 29:9—30:30

VAYELEKH

Moses said to the Children of Israel:

"I am a hundred and twenty years old this day. I can no longer move about; and the Lord has told me, 'You shall not cross over this Jordan.' Be strong and of good courage, fear not; for the Lord your God goes with you. He will not fail you, nor forsake you."

Then Moses called Joshua, and said to him before all Israel: "Be strong and of good courage, for you shall go forth with His people into the land which the Lord promised their forefathers; and you shall cause them to inherit it. The Lord will lead you. He will be with you. Do not fear, nor be dismayed."

And Moses wrote the Law—the Torah—and gave it to the priests, the sons of Levi who carried the Holy Ark, and to all the elders of Israel.

Then Moses commanded them: "At the end of every seven years, during Sukkot, you shall read aloud the Torah before all Israel."

When Moses finished writing the Torah, he ordered the Levites to place it beside the Ark of the Covenant of the Lord, and to assemble all the elders and the officers, that he might speak to them.

Deuteronomy 31:1—30

HAAZINU

האזינו

Moses bade farewell in a lofty and noble poem. He called upon heaven and earth as witnesses to Israel's acceptance of the Covenant with God. And Moses said:

"Remember the days of old,
Think back to the years of long ago;
Ask your father and he will tell you,
Ask your elders and they will tell you.
When the Most High gave the nations
their inheritance,
He took for Himself the people of Israel,
Jacob for His very own share.
He found him in a desert land.
He protected him and cared for him
As an eagle gently wakes its young
To teach them how to fly,
Spreading its wings to catch them when
they tire,
So did the Lord watch over him
And lead him through desert and fire."

On that very same day, the Lord spoke to Moses: "Moses, my son, ascend the Mountain of Nebo which overlooks Canaan. There you will go to your eternal rest. For though you will see the land which I promised to Abraham, Isaac, and Jacob, you yourself will never enter it."

Moses bowed his head before the will of the Lord.

Deuteronomy 32:1—52

V-ZOT HA-BRAKHAH

וזאת הברכה

The final sidra of the Five Books of Moses contains the last words of the great leader who guided his people to the Promised Land. He blessed each one of the tribes of Israel, saying:

"The Lord came from Sinai,
He loves all people who are just and upright.
May Reuben live long; may God help Judah in his battles.
Let Levi protect the Urim and Tummim, and
May Benjamin live free from fear.
Let blessings rain on Joseph's head: his tribes of
Ephraim and Manasseh are his stalwart warriors.
Zebulun will be a sea-merchant, and Issachar
Will study at home. Gad will receive
A large portion, for he was daring in battle.
Dan is strong as a lion and Naphtali—
He's content with his lot.
Asher is bound to be a favorite, and he will have
Strength his whole life long."

The blessings over, Moses went up to Mount Nebo. God showed him the Promised Land,

and the portions He would give to each of the tribes.

There, on top of the mountain, Moses was taken by the Lord, and there he died. To this day no one knows where his grave is. He was one hundred and twenty years old when he died, but his eyes were clear and his body strong.

The Children of Israel wept for Moses for thirty days, and then the mourning period was ended. And Joshua prepared to take Moses' place.

But never since Moses has there been a prophet in Israel like Moses, a man to whom God had spoken face to face.

Deuteronomy 33:1—34:12

ALL ABOUT THE TORAH

Writing a Sefer Torah

The Sefer Torah must always be written by hand. Today, as for countless past generations, the Holy Scroll is prepared with painstaking care by a Sofer, or scribe, especially trained in Jewish law and traditions for his sacred task.

Here are some of the main steps followed by a Sofer in writing a Sefer Torah:

1. For parchment, the Sofer may use only the hide of a clean animal (one that, according to the Torah, is kosher to eat). With a sharp point, he draws lines on the parchment, dividing each piece into 3 to 8 sections, with 42 to 72 lines for each section.

These tools are used in writing a Torah Scroll. Here you see the inkwell, the reeds and their case, quills, and sinews (of kosher animals) for sewing parchment sheets together.

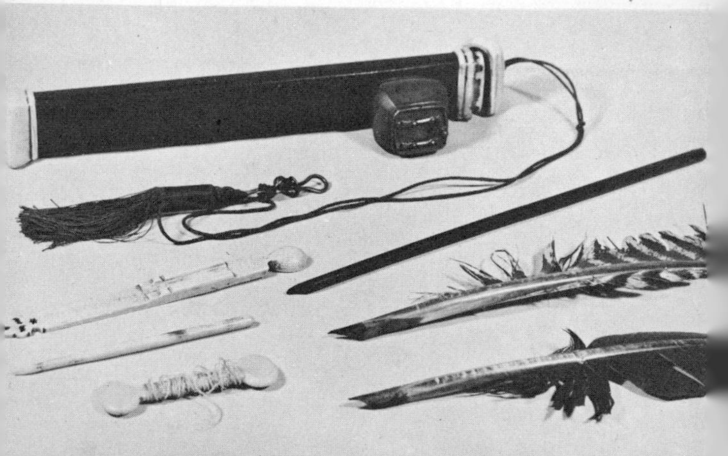

ואין מחריד יככה יהוה בשחין מצרים ובעפלי
ובגרב ובחרס אשר לא תוכל להרפא יככה
יהוה בשגעון ובעורון ובתמהון לבב והיי
ממשש בצהרים כאשר ימשש העור באפל
ולא תצליח את דרכיך והיית אך עשוק וגזו
כל הימים ואין מושיע אשה תארש ואיש א
ישגלנה בית תבנה ולא תשב בו כרם תטע ול
תחללנו שורך טבוח לעיניך ולא תאכל ממ
חמרך גזול מלפניך ולא ישוב לך צאנך נתנו

he *sofer* uses a special script. The decorative little crowns, alled *tagin,* may be used on only seven letters of the leph Bet. The *sofer* may not write from memory and he ust pronounce each word before writing it.

2. A Sefer Torah must be written in special black ink only. The pen is a feather of a clean (kosher) fowl, with the tip sliced off at an angle, and the point slit. This writing tool can shape thick or thin strokes, as required.

3. The Sofer uses a special script. He may not write even one word from memory and he must pronounce each word before writing it.

4. Only seven letters of the Aleph-Bet may have decorative little crowns called *Tagin.*

5. Some sections are written in a special form. The Song of the Red Sea *(Exodus 15)* is arranged like bricks in a wall, a reminder of how God split the waters so that our ancestors

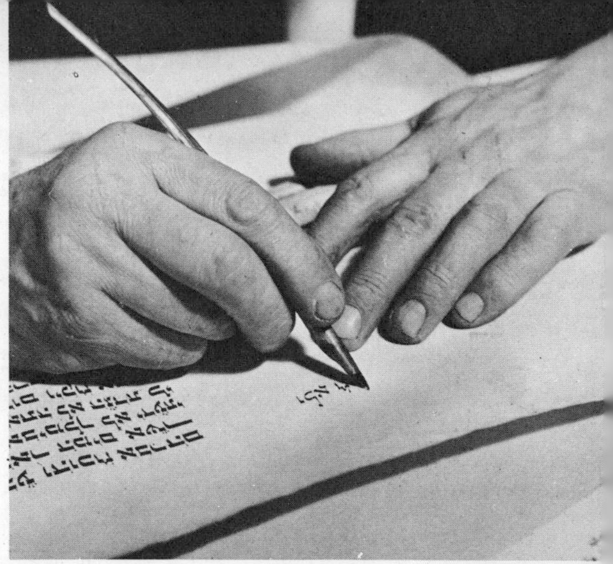

When a scribe *(sofer)*, writes a Torah Scroll, he rul guide lines with the blunt edge of a knife, and divides ea parchment sheet into sections. Every Torah Scroll must b entirely hand-written.

might pass unharmed. The last few lines of the Sefer Torah are left unfinished. They will be filled in at a synagogue ceremony called the "Completion of the Sefer Torah," the *Siyyum Ha-Sefer.*

6. The sheets are sewn together with sinews of animals (kosher), and woven into long threads. The sewing may not be visible on the face of the Sefer Torah.

In preparing a Sefer Torah, the scribe *(sofer)* sews the beginning and end sheets of parchment to two wooden rollers, each known as an *Etz Hayyim* (Tree of Life).

7. The Scroll is attached to two wooden rollers, each called the "Tree of Life," the *Etz Hayyim*.

A silver-gilt Torah crown *(keter Torah)* made in Breslau, Germany, in 1750, showing biblical scenes.

Keter Torah

Over the upper ends of the *Atzey Hayyim* we place the *Keter Torah,* the "crown of the Torah." It is usually wrought of silver and adorned with little bells, and is one of the scroll's chief ornaments.

The wooden rollers (the *Atzey Hayyim* or "trees of life") on which the Scrolls of the *Torah* are wound are made of hard wood with handles of ivory and have flat round tops and bottoms to support the edges of the rolled-up Scroll. The Torah, too, is called the *Etz Hayyim,* the "tree of life."

Mantle of the Law

The Mantle of the Law covers the holy scroll when it is not in use. Thus we protect

The Holy Scroll containing the Five Books of Moses is the most sacred possession of the Jewish people.

Chinese Torah Ark from the Kai-Fung-Foo synagogue. Th Ark dates from the 17th century.

the Torah from dust or injury. Shaped to slip over the Torah when it is rolled up, the mantle is open at the bottom and closed at the top, except for two round openings to allow the scroll handles to pass through. It is made of embroidered silk or satin which has never been used for any other purpose before. Old worn-out mantles, like the Scroll and all objects associated with it, are stored away, for they are too sacred to be discarded or used for anything else.

Hoshen

When the Torah is taken out of the Ark, we see its beautiful breastplate suspended by a chain from the top of the rollers. Lions, eagles,

Silver Torah breastplate, with figures of Moses and Aaron, made in Poland in the 18th century. At the bottom you can see hands raised in priestly blessing.

This Torah Ark of Cong. Beth Elohim, Charleston, S. C., is a replica of the one destroyed by fire in 1838. The original Ark was built in 1799.

flags, and the Magen David are its chief decorations. In the center of the breastplate there is frequently a tiny Ark whose doors are in the form of the two tablets of the Law. The lower part of the breastplate has a place where small plates may be inserted. The name of one of the Jewish festivals is engraved on each plate, to be displayed on the holiday or Sabbath on which the scroll is used.

Aron Ha-Kodesh

We keep the scrolls of the *Torah* in the *Aron Ha-Kodesh,* or "holy ark." This chest or closet is named after the *Aron Ha-Brit,* the Ark of the Covenant, which held the Tablets of the Ten Commandments when our ancestors crossed the desert. The Aron Ha-Kodesh is placed against the wall of the synagogue facing east or toward Jerusalem. It is often made of costly carved wood or marble, and it is crowned by the tablets of the Law.

Parokhet

Just as the Children of Israel while wandering in the desert hung a curtain before the Ark of the Covenant, so do we follow their ancient example in many of our synagogues today. The *Parokhet,* or curtain, is made of satin, velvet,

Torah Ark curtain made in Germany and dated 1768.

or other fine material, and is richly embroidered, usually with the Ten Commandments.

Yad

The pointer of silver or olive wood which is used to guide the reading of the Torah is called the *Yad*, or "hand." Shaped like a staff, its end is narrow and in the form of a closed fist with the forefinger outstretched. When the Torah is rolled, the Yad is hung by a chain over the Atzey Hayyim, and rests on the silver breastplate.

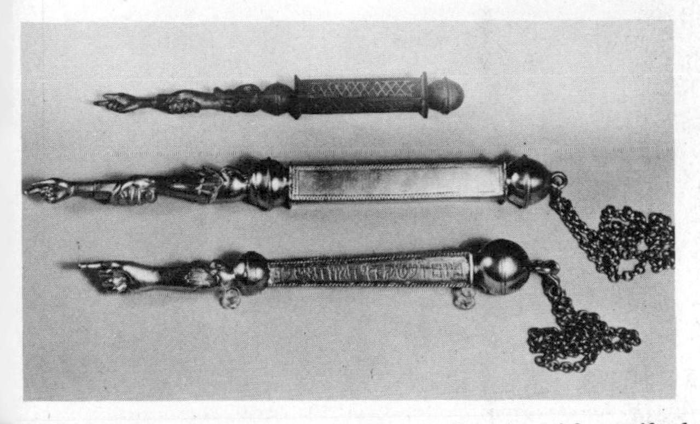

Torah pointers (one of wood, two of silver), with motif of a dolphin head and hand, made in Eastern Europe in the early 19th century. The pointer *(yad)* is used because one should not touch the Scroll with the bare fingers.

A pair of Torah headpieces *(rimmonim)* made of silver and cast in Amsterdam, Holland, in the early 17th century.

Rimmonim

This is the Hebrew name for "pomegranates," and is used for the ornaments placed on the Atzey Hayyim of the Torah. Formerly, they were shaped like pomegranates but later were generally in tower form. Rimmonim originally decorated the robe of the High Priest, on which bells and pomegranates were placed alternately (*Exodus* 39:25-26).

Sections of an embroidered mappah; Germany, 19th century. A "mappah" is the sash which is tied around the middle of the Torah before it is replaced in the Ark.

PHOTOGRAPH CREDITS

The Jewish Museum (Jewish Theological Seminary). Photos by Frank J. Darmstaedter. 98, 102, 104, 105, 106, 108, 109, 110, 111.

Herbert S. Sonnenfeld, 103.

Three Lions Inc., 100, 101.